BOOK ENDO

Jim Woodroof: This is a very good book: The title invites, the contents inform; the arrangement is clear and concise. It contains personal experiences that draw the reader in and put flesh on theory. It has the right basis—the Bible; the correct message—Jesus. It calls for the required response—faith, demonstrated in a change of mind and baptism and sealed by the Holy Spirit. And it is convicting: it asks each believer this riveting question: "Are you going into all the world" to fulfill His Great Commission? I recommend we follow the Heavenly Star as described in this book. Thus, by God's grace, the reader can 'stand before God without guilt or fear.'

Dr. Anthony Wood, Assistant Director, River City Ministry, North Little Rock AR: Many of us have been blessed by The Book of Romans as we have shared the Good News of Jesus. Jim has done us a great favor in bringing together years of wisdom and personal experiences in a "Roman's approach" to Gospel sharing. Study this book! It will not only strengthen personal faith in your own spiritual journey but also inspire and prepare you to help others come to faith in Jesus. Though you may not consider yourself to have the gift of evangelism, this little book makes possible the opportunity for every Christian to learn how to effectively share the Gospel.

Terry Rush: As you read Jim's book, welcome to the yearn of God. Be in awe of His intense reach. Prepare your heart to respond in faith action. You and God . . . a powerful match . . . to invite others to a new life!

Wes Woodell: One should enjoy rare and rich food slowly, and Heaven's Star is no exception. Jim Woodell's background includes a faithful and fruitful forty years of service in evangelistic ministry in addition to a thorough knowledge of the Scriptures. When a man like Jim puts pen to paper to record some of the greatest lessons he's learned in life, the wise should read and read well. Like all rare and rich food, this book is not to be devoured quickly. Ingest it slowly, savor the flavor, and enjoy a hearty meal that's meant to be shared with others.

William Tucker, Elder: As a disciple of Jesus you are an ambassador of Christ's Kingdom and a minister of reconciliation. Jesus has entrusted you with the powerful message that salvation is a free gift to those in Christ. He wants to make his appeal to the lost world through you. Are you prepared to make that appeal? This book will equip you to share the incredible good news using Paul's Letter to the Romans. Utilizing Romans, Chapters 4-8, Jim Woodell masterfully sets forth a unique method of sharing the gospel. I first encountered the Romans Approach to the gospel in 1974. It was powerful and effective then and still is today.

Claire Shirley (13 Years Old): The book, Heaven's Star gives people a way to become closer to God as they help others do the same.

CHECK THIS ANCIENT GPS

HEAVEN'S STAR

JIM WOODELL

ISBN: 978-1-4782-8100-9

Library of Congress Control Number: 2012912622

CONTENTS

PREFACE

My dad pointed me toward God from birth. He was far from a perfect man, but he believed God provided his grace for the imperfect and he passed that down to his family. I look back at my life and see signs of God drawing me to himself: at age ten, 20, 21, 30 and other times. Each of these life changes (perspective changes) had their own unique contribution to my walk with God. It was not that I was dishonest and then became honest as I took each step. Rather, I was and am a God seeker and know now, more than ever, that seeking God will always require changes in my life, both in thought and practice.

In the pages of this book I share some of my own personal experiences and then a study of Paul's letter to the Romans, a book that reassures (Romans 8:1 " . . . now no condemnation for those that are in Christ . . . ") and challenges (Romans 12:1 " . . . offer your body as a living sacrifice . . .). In 1972, one of my life changing years, I discovered the power of presenting Christ (the gospel, Romans 1:16-17), and Christ alone to people. From then until now, when I have opportunity, I present a study from Romans that is Christ centered and I urge people to respond to Him as LORD. I have witnessed a number of individuals give their lives to Christ after just one study.

God did not send Christ into the world to tell sinners what to do for Him; He sent Jesus into the world to show us what he has done for us! This book is about God's provision for the lost; what He has done for sinners. The study of Romans 4-8 will give you a plan to use when you have an opportunity to sit down with someone to share the good news. Based on my own personal experiences and my study of Romans this book is divided into two parts:

Section 1 is "Preparation."

Section 2 is "A Plan."

We see Jesus, who was made a little lower than the angels, now crowned with glory and honor because he suffered death, so that by the grace of God he might taste death for everyone (Hebrews 2:9).

ACKNOWLEDGEMENT

My passion to inspire others to share the gospel has been my motivation in writing this book. I am indebted to many who have provided insight and practical advice. Foremost among these is my wife of 50 years, Geraldine. Always ready to help and responding quickly to the editorial part of this production was Terry Rush, Jim Woodroof, David Bowman, Anthony Wood and, my son, Wes. I am also indebted to the Board of Directors of River City Ministry who allowed me a three month sabbatical for this project. I also want to mention the staff of RCM that serves so faithfully every day. Witnessing Dr. Anthony Wood lift up Christ in the inner city has been a blessing. Thank you all. Thanks also to William Tucker and the Brentwood Hills Church of Christ in Nashville, TN who invited me to share The Romans Approach with them (six sessions on one Sunday), and then encouraged me to refine the material and get it into print.

Also, thanks to K.C. Moser whose books **The Gist of Romans** and **Way of Salvation** changed my life in the early seventies. Although he was gone from this life he spoke to me powerfully.

This book is launched with a prayer that many will learn a simple, but excellent way to introduce others to our LORD.

INTRODUCTION

Lost! At the age of four I was lost. Literally. Being the youngest of five children I was the only child at home with my mom. We lived in the country. As I played in the yard one morning a group of hogs wandered by and our dogs set out in hot pursuit of them. Of course I followed. It wasn't long before I didn't know where I was! Even so I continued to follow the dogs deeper into the woods. Later my mom noticed my absence and set out to find me but I was long gone! Soon the word spread and the community turned out in force to comb the woods. Luckily, a neighbor, Thomas Phillips, did find me and I rode out to my mother's arms on a horse with another neighbor, Vance Peavy. You don't forget the names of those who find you when you are lost.

When I was in my early thirties a friend and I went into the Ozark Mountains to do some scouting for deer sign. We pulled into a logging road, parked and set out to scout. We plodded up hills and walked down into some valleys and around other hills. After awhile we decided to go back to the truck, but we realized, to our dismay, that we did not know where it was. After wandering around for some time we finally heard highway noise and, with great relief, went to it. There we found some campers. After confessing our plight to them they gave us a ride back to our truck, about five miles away. We were lost!

Today I use a GPS and I don't get lost. If properly set and followed, it will take you home. The same is true in our spiritual journey. In the pages that follow I will share with you how you can set your spiritual GPS and know you are on your way home. You will also be equipped to help others set their GPS.

MY STORY

I grew up in a family of seven children. Our dad was 65 years old when I was born, but he wasn't done; two more followed me. Dad was 72 when the youngest came along.

I thought of my dad as a very religious man. He had been a deacon in the Baptist Church; he saw to it that we were in our pew every Sunday, as well as often leading our family in home devotions. With seven rowdy children, the only reason dad would have tackled such a challenge had to be his strong convictions! As a result of his spiritual leading, I grew up believing Jesus Christ to be "the only begotten Son of God."

A near-by Methodist Church proved to be the most convenient place of worship for our family. At the age of ten I professed my faith and joined the Methodist Church, beginning my search for God.

When I was 14, dad died, leaving mom with four children at home. The older three had joined the military. Three years later she signed for me to join the U.S. Navy—two days after I turned 17. After a couple of years, I re-enlisted for six more years. While home on leave during this enlistment, I became reacquainted with a beautiful young lady whose family I had known most of my life. After dating several months, we decided to get married. She and her parents were members of the Freewill Baptist Church. Through their influence I was immersed into that church. I had felt for some time that God was calling me to preach. My first effort to fulfill this calling was at the Oak Grove Freewill Baptist Church in 1962 when I attempted to preach at the evening service. Attempted is the key word.

Oddly enough, though actively trying to connect with God, I still felt empty—I wasn't satisfied with my relationship with him. So, I continued to search for ways to draw closer to him, such as church attendance, and sharing my faith.

In 1963, just over a year after I joined and became active in the Freewill Baptist Church, a friend who had recently been baptized into the Church of Christ challenged my salvation. He shared scriptures such as Mark 16:15-16, where Jesus told the apostles,

> *"Go into all the world and preach the good news to all creation. Whoever believes and is baptized will be saved, but whoever does not believe will be condemned."*

He showed me Acts 2:38 where Peter powerfully preached the good news, then boldly declared the audience guilty of crucifying

Christ! Cut to the heart with guilt, they asked, "Brothers, what shall we do?"

Peter replied, "Repent and be baptized, every one of you, in the name of Jesus Christ for the forgiveness of your sins. And you will receive the gift of the Holy Spirit."

This really challenged me! It revealed in concrete terms what God was calling me to do, which was to place myself under Christ's authority and be baptized into him. The blessings promised were forgiveness and the gift of the Holy Spirit. However, my understanding of how to share Christ was flawed. For years I taught certain steps to be followed to become a Christian, with barely a mention of Jesus. I emphasized the right church with the right name, and the correct acts of worship—a formula. I saw this formula as the answer for the lost.

My perception of the gospel message began to change only after I graduated from college with a degree in Bible. This is how it came about: At every opportunity, my brother-in-law, Gerry, and I discussed Scripture. He has a Master's Degree in English and dearly loves debating. We covered the steps (the formula), the right church, and the correct acts of worship—Gerry was neither moved nor impressed.

Then my brother, John, came to visit; Gerry happened to be there also. It wasn't long before he and I began our usual lively discussion of the Word. John was quiet while we disputed, then broke a temporary lull by asking Gerry, "What do think about Jesus?"

He had our undivided attention. Gerry responded, "Oh, I believe he lived, and died on a cross." John then asked, "Do you realize he died on that cross for you?" Gerry became quiet. John continued to present Jesus, connecting completely with our brother-in-law, something I had never been able to do. John's approach opened my eyes to my rule-laden, powerless approach to soul-winning. My brother-in-law was obviously convicted, so I jumped in and asked, "Gerry, do you believe Jesus was buried, and raised from the dead three days later?"

"Yes, I do believe that."

I then asked, "Do you believe Jesus is the Son of God?"

"Yes, I believe Jesus is the Son of God."

The three of us drove to the church building where I preached and Gerry was baptized immediately. I know God forgave Gerry and freely gave him the Holy Spirit that night, just as he forgave those on the day of Pentecost and blessed them with his indwelling Spirit. (Acts 2:38)

Gerry, however, wasn't the only one to "see the light" that evening. Through the Holy Spirit's teaching, I saw the profound power of simply sharing Jesus Christ. I saw Heaven's Star and set my GPS that night.

I pray that the study that follows will help you in your journey. I have personally witnessed several opening their hearts to the Lord within two hours of beginning a study of Romans. The *secret* to setting your own GPS is revealed in the pages that follow.

Notes

SECTION I

Notes

PREPARATION

Jesus described the discovery of the kingdom of heaven and salvation in the parables called the "Hidden Treasure and the Pearl" (Matthew 13:44-45). Scripture records it like this:

> *"The kingdom of heaven is like treasure hidden in a field. When a man found it, he hid it again, and then in his joy went and sold all he had and bought that field.*

> *"Again, the kingdom of heaven is like a merchant looking for fine pearls. When he found one of great value, he went away and sold everything he had and bought it.*

If you have made this discovery, you will be blessed to share the treasure with others. If you have not made this discovery Section II will be more for you. Your personal salvation is worth more than all of the material possessions you will ever own. According to Jesus your salvation is worth more than the whole world (Matthew 16:26).

Perhaps you are saying, "I would like to share my faith, but I'm just not ready." This section on preparation is for you and Section II will give you a plan to work with. Paul instructed Timothy in 2 Timothy 2:1-2, *"You then, my son, be strong in the grace that is in Christ Jesus. And the things you have heard me say in the presence of many witnesses entrust to reliable men who will also be qualified to teach others."*

Reliable Christians are instructed by Paul to share with others, who are qualified, to teach others the things that Paul taught. Who are the "reliable?" Those that you can depend on. The reliable are those who have discovered the kingdom of God and have in their *hearts set apart Christ as Lord.* It is only at this point that we are prepared to give a reason for the hope that we have and to do it with sincerity. As we share with others we are to do it with gentleness and respect as we keep our conscience clear. Only the reliable are qualified to teach others.

Hear Peter from 1 Peter 3:15-16:

> *But in your hearts set apart Christ as Lord. Always be prepared to give an answer to everyone who asks you to give the reason for the hope that you have. But do this with gentleness and respect, keeping a clear conscience, so that those who speak maliciously against your good behavior in Christ may be ashamed of their slander.*

Are people asking you to give the reason for your hope? Peter assumes people will ask. Could it be that my lifestyle does not reflect the living presence of Jesus? Could it be that I live in the comfort of a circle of Christians and have no contact with the unsaved? Do I need to make some changes so I will be in contact with people who will ask? Do I need to make some lifestyle changes to more effectively reflect the living presence of Jesus? Why aren't people asking?

In John 4 Jesus shared the following:

> *Do you not say, 'Four months more and then the harvest'? I tell you, open your eyes and look at the fields! They are ripe for harvest. Even now the reaper draws his wages, even now he harvests the crop for eternal life, so that the sower and the reaper may be glad together. Thus the saying 'One sows and another reaps' is true. I sent you to reap what you have not worked for. Others have done the hard work, and you have reaped the benefits of their labor."*

God is sending us to "reap" what we have not worked for. Jesus has done the hard work. He left heaven, suffered persecution on earth, died on the cross, was buried in a borrowed tomb and then raised from the dead to live forever. Through the Romans letter God calls us to live under the Lordship of Christ.

If you are willing to talk about Jesus Christ, you will discover what follows to be very effective. You can bring glory to God and experience joy by letting him use you to spread his word. How wonderful that our God will use clay vessels (us) in his work.

BETTER THAN A GPS

Something better than a GPS is a personal guide; someone who is familiar with the territory, who has walked over the lay of the land and who can give you personal guidance and help when you need it. In this spiritual journey we are on that is JESUS.

CHAPTER 1

✳ ——•—— ✳

KEEP YOUR EYE ON THE BALL

"Let us fix our eyes on Jesus, the author and perfecter of our faith, who for the joy set before him endured the cross, scorning its shame, and sat down at the right hand of the throne of God." (Hebrews 12:2)

THE MESSAGE IS JESUS!

Our son, Wes, started playing Tee Ball at age 5. Using something like a light weight plastic ball that was hollow and placing it on top of a stake (like an over-sized golf tee) the batter was given a plastic bat and told to hit the ball off the tee. He tried. After a number of attempts, sometimes swinging over and sometimes swinging under he would hit the ball. He went from Tee Ball to Teeny League then to Little League. At every level the key to hitting the ball was to keep your eye on it as you swung the bat. By the time he got to Pony League he was hitting home run after home run. He had learned the secret of keeping his eye on the ball.

Religion does not define Christianity. Christianity is about a relationship. It's all about JESUS. Whatever we share, and however we share the gospel, we must magnify Jesus. It's so easy to get side-tracked, to focus on "what" instead of "who." It is too easy to campaign on behalf of a church or a particular doctrine or plan, and fail to share the good news—Jesus!

Just like in baseball it is called "keeping your eye on the ball." We must be sure we present the Son of God who said, *"But I, when I am lifted up from the earth, will draw all men to myself" (John 12:32).* Keep your eye on Jesus. After all, the essential question that really matters, when talking about salvation, is *"What will you let Jesus do with you?"*

"Moses said to God, 'Suppose I go to the Israelites and say to them, 'The God of your fathers has sent me to you,' and they ask me, 'What is his name?' Then what shall I tell them? God said to Moses, "I AM WHO I AM. This is what you are to say to the Israelites: 'I AM has sent me to you'" (Exodus 3:13-14).

Seven times in John's gospel Jesus proclaims himself to be the "I AM" who is God Almighty, the ONE who terrified Moses with the assignment of going back to Egypt to deliver his people from bondage.

We must share the great "I AM" with others!

THE SEVEN "I AM'S" IN THE GOSPEL OF JOHN

1. John 6:35: *"Then Jesus declared, 'I am the bread of life. He who comes to me will never go hungry, and he who believes in me will never be thirsty.'"* Jesus taught his disciple to pray for their daily bread. Bread sustains life and Jesus is that bread.

2. John 8:12: *"I am the light of the world. Whoever follows me will never walk in darkness, but will have the light of life."* In this same chapter Jesus declares in verse 58: *"I tell you*

the truth, before Abraham was born, I am!" It is Jesus that illuminates the path that we should walk on.

3. John 10:7: *"I tell you the truth, I am the gate for the sheep."* Again in John 10:9, *"I am the gate; whoever enters through me will be saved. He will come in and go out, and find pasture."* Jesus did not say that he was "a gate." He is "the gate" that we must enter through.

4. John 10:11: *"I am the good shepherd. The good shepherd lays down his life for the sheep."* Again in John 10:14-15, *"I am the good shepherd; I know my sheep and my sheep know me—just as the Father knows me and I know the Father—and I lay down my life for the sheep."* Jesus laid down his life for "his sheep." All of those who accept the "good shepherd" are his sheep. It is by his life that we are saved from damnation.

5. John 11:25-26: *"I am the resurrection and the life. He who believes in me will live, even though he dies; and whoever lives and believes in me will never die."* Do you believe this?" Really? Do I believe this? Notice that Jesus did not say he would be resurrected, he said, *"I am the resurrection."*

6. John 14:6: *"I am the way and the truth and the life. No one comes to the Father except through me."* Again, Jesus is not "a" way but "the way." He is also "the truth," and "the life." There is no other source for eternal life than Jesus.

7. John 15:1-2: *"I am the true vine, and my Father is the gardener. He cuts off every branch in me that bears no fruit,*

while every branch that does bear fruit he prunes so that it will be even more fruitful." Jesus is the vine that Christians are attached to for eternal life. Christians must bear the fruit of that relationship.

Questions:

1. Why is it important to make Jesus the message?

2. Give an example of focusing on the "what" instead of the "who" of our salvation.

3. Which of the seven "I Am's" of John is most meaningful to you, and why?

4. Do you really believe that Jesus is "the resurrection?"

CHAPTER 2

JESUS IS FOR LOSERS

*"**Come** to me, all you who are weary and burdened, and I will give you rest. **Take** my yoke upon you and **learn** from me, for I am gentle and humble in heart, and you will find rest for your souls. For my yoke is easy and my burden is light."* (Matthew 11:28-30)

THE GREAT INVITATION

When we share Jesus with others we are simply extending the invitation that he himself shared with the people of his personal ministry. It is His invitation. There are three parts to the invitation and the focus is on him. Notice:

- Jesus said, **"Come to <u>me</u> . . . <u>I</u> will give you rest."**

- Jesus said to those who answered his invitation to come, **"Take <u>my</u> yoke upon you . . . "**

- Thirdly, Jesus said, **"Learn from <u>me</u> . . . and you will find rest . . . "**

The invitation is to the "weary and burdened." Jesus offers to take that load onto himself. When my oldest grandson, Josh, was about five years old he walked into the living room with a belt buckled around his upper arms and chest. He announced with a very confident voice, "I'm going to break this belt!" He then took a deep breath and strained until his face was beet red, but with disappointment, turned and left the room the belt still intact. He had obviously been influenced by watching super heroes on TV.

Often we too struggle with problems that overwhelm us. Peter wrote in 1 Peter 5:6-7:

> *"Humble yourselves, therefore, under God's mighty hand, that he may lift you up in due time. Cast all your anxiety on him because he cares for you."*

Jesus used a yoke of oxen, so familiar to his audience, to illustrate his invitation. He invited all to join him in the yoke, as younger oxen were yoked together with older, stronger, more experienced animals to learn from them. When we team up with Jesus, he'll bear the majority of the load, give us rest, and teach us as we walk alongside him. This is where the "abundant life" is found. It is all about Jesus! The greatest weight we bear in life is that of our own sins, and it is too much for us to lift! Only Jesus has the power to lift this burden or break this bond.

Only Jesus has the power and authority to forgive sins. As Jesus was in a house teaching a crowd of people four men lowered a paralyzed man, lying on a mat, down through the roof to get to him. Jesus said, "Your sins are forgiven. Take up your mat and walk," and the paralyzed man did. The people gathered there immediately criticized Jesus saying, "Who can forgive sins but God alone" (Mark 2:1-12). True. Only Almighty God can forgive sins, and Jesus did. This man was a loser, but not in the way society believed him to be. He was the biggest loser in the room that day, because his friends brought him to Jesus and he lost the weight of his sins.

Another time Jesus was invited into a Pharisees house to eat, a woman that is described as having led "a sinful life" showed up. She stood behind Jesus as he reclined at the table and washed his feet with her flowing tears. She kissed his feet and dried them with her long hair. He said to her, "Your sins are forgiven!" (Luke 7:36-50) Jesus has the authority to forgive sins. This woman was the biggest loser in the room, but not in the way the Pharisees thought. She came to Jesus, and lost the weight of her sin.

I pray that we will all be losers—people who come to Jesus, and lose the weight of our sins. We are to first **come to Jesus**, then **take his yoke**, and finally **learn from him**. Many want to **learn,** then **come** and **take**. Others want to **come, learn** and **take**; however God's way is the only way that will work. We are to first come to Jesus, and then learn from him by taking his yoke. Love should be the drawing force to get someone to come to Jesus. Paul said, *"Knowledge puffs up, but love builds up" (1 Corinthians 8:1b).*

Accept His order of the invitation: *Come to Jesus—Take his yoke—Learn from Him.*

Questions:

1.   What does it mean to "come" to Jesus?

2.   Why is it important that we take his "yoke" upon us?

3. How do we "learn from him?"

4. What is the "rest" that is promised?

5. Why is the "rest" mentioned twice in the invitation?

6. To share Jesus with others I must first overcome my own paralysis, take up my mat, and get moving. I can only share the invitation of Jesus if I have, first, accepted it. Do you believe Jesus has the authority to forgive sins? Your sins?

Wes Woodell's Testimony

Sitting across the table from me, he said, "I'm about to share with you the most powerful thing in the world." Apparently the bit of skepticism I felt showed on my face, because he followed up: "I'm serious. I'm about to share the most powerful thing in the world with you—the gospel of Jesus Christ!"

My dad proceeded to walk me through the outline lying before him, and after we finished he folded it in half and handed it to me instructing me to use it with someone else just as he had with me.

I had given my life to Christ only a few weeks prior to this encounter, and would soon find ample opportunity to utilize this new tool my dad had given me.

About a month later, I sat among peers at a Bible study for USF students in Tampa, FL. God had been working in this particular campus ministry, and many new Christians sat in the room telling stories of repentance and how God had been blessing them in Jesus.

One young man named Brent was new to the group, and this was his first Bible study. Hearing the stories of life change and God's grace from people his own age had an obvious impact on him, because at the end of the study Brent shared how he too wanted what we had. This was an opportunity.

I approached Brent after the closing prayer and said something like this: "I really appreciated what you had to say. Someone recently taught me something that might help—can I share it with you?"

"Sure," he responded. I grabbed my Bible with my folded copy of that outline my dad had given me in it, and after moving to a quieter part of the house with Brent and another buddy from the college ministry, opened it up.

I was *so* nervous.

I remember my hand shaking as I unfolded that outline. I remember not knowing it very well. I remember stuttering and stammering through the text. I remember feeling like I was messing it up badly. I remember honestly wondering if I was going to be partly responsible for damning this young man in addition to his own sin.

I remember wanting to run away—it was a simply awful presentation . . .

. . . But God made it effective.

At the end of our study, Brent expressed that he wanted to follow Jesus.

Our entire group drove to the church building that night, and I had the privilege of baptizing Brent into Jesus Christ. It was an amazing experience—I had only just been baptized myself and barely knew anything, but I did know Jesus was pleased that night.

Since then God has continually blessed me with opportunities to meet and share with many like Brent.

I am *still* inadequate, but have learned that the power is in the message—not the messenger! Our job is to share the message and keep sharing.

If you have a copy of the Romans Approach to Reaching the Lost in your hands, I have something to tell you: you have in your possession the most powerful thing in the world.

I'm serious. It's the most powerful thing in the world—the gospel of Jesus Christ!

CHAPTER 3

AS YOU ARE GOING INTO ALL THE WORLD

"Therefore go and make disciples of all nations, baptizing them in the name of the Father and of the Son and of the Holy Spirit, and teaching them to obey everything I have commanded you. And surely I am with you always to the very end of the age." (Matthew 28:19-20)

Jesus expected those who answered his invitation to share their knowledge with others. Just after his death, burial and resurrection, and just prior to ascending back into heaven, Jesus urged his disciples to share the good news with others. Because of the scope of this charge it is referred to as The Great Commission.

He said:

- **Go** (or has been translated more accurately, "As you are going into all the world).

- **Make disciples**

- **Baptizing them and teaching them to observe everything commanded** (Teaching everything commanded includes making disciples)

The charge Jesus gave to his disciples and that is passed on down to us is to introduce individuals to Jesus and HIS invitation, to make disciples of them, and lead them to salvation. We must teach enough truth to a lost person so that he or she comes to know Jesus and how to become His disciple. However, Scripture does not require that we teach all that is commanded before baptizing a lost man or woman. Teaching them to obey everything commanded FOLLOWS baptism.

Note that since *"faith comes from hearing the message"* (*Romans 10:17*), the amount of time spent teaching before baptism will vary between individuals. The spark of faith simply takes longer to ignite in some people more than others. Remember that the Holy Spirit will do his work in his own time in a person's heart (John 16:8-11)—we are the message-bearers, watching for the spark of faith.

The commission from Jesus is for Christians today! Jesus told the apostles to be teaching the new converts *"to obey everything I have commanded you."* The Lord had just commanded his apostles to *"Go and make disciples of all nations . . . "* These followers of Christ understood this to be a command, a charge given them, as evidenced by Peter's declaration in Acts 10:42: *"He commanded us to preach to the people and to testify that he is the one whom God appointed as judge of the living and the dead."*

Jesus gave a clear "mission statement" to his disciples in Acts 1:8:

> *"You will receive power when the Holy Spirit comes on you; and you will be my witnesses in Jerusalem, and in all Judea and Samaria, and to the ends of the earth."*

They were to start in Jerusalem, then go into all Judea and all of Samaria then to the ends of the earth. The word translated "all nations" comes from the Greek word *ethnos* from which we get the word *ethnic*. This is a word to describe people groups (red, yellow, black and white). So, the Great Commission is not only being fulfilled by missionaries going overseas, but it is also individual Christians reaching out to friends, neighbors and family.

Note this interesting comparison between the Great Invitation and the Great Commission. From my experience, I know this parallel is true. Notice:

THE GREAT INVITATION
AND THE GREAT COMMISSION

The Great Invitation	The Great Commission
COME	GO
TAKE	MAKE DISCIPLES
LEARN	BAPTIZE AND TEACH TO OBEY EVERYTHING COMMANDED

Those who *Come, Take,* and *Learn* are to *Go, Make Disciples.* We make disciples *BY* baptizing them and teaching them to obey all that Christ commanded. Only those who have accepted the Great Invitation are charged with implementing the Great Commission. No man or woman can go to all nations, make disciples, baptize and teach everything commanded who has not accepted the Lord Jesus Christ, shouldered his yoke, and is continually learning from him through the Spirit. Every disciple of Jesus is charged to pass the word along. Declare what you have seen and heard, not as a creed, but as a living experience.

Who is a disciple of Jesus Christ? This question is addressed by Jesus in John 8:31-32:

> *"If you hold to my teaching, you are really my disciples. Then you will know the truth, and the truth will set you free."*

So a disciple is one who holds to the teachings of Jesus. While on a mission trip to Scotland I met a young man who was a steward on a luxury liner. He told of the time he was out on the deck of the ship one night alone, observing the stars and thinking about his relationship with God. He said in that moment he surrendered his heart to God and asked that Jesus be his Lord and Savior. In an attempt to lead him closer to the Lord I asked, "Do you believe all that you know in the teachings of Jesus?" After a pause he responded, "Yes, and I even believe what I do not yet know!" A disciple of Christ is one who is a disciplined learner; a student of the Bible.

We can share the gospel with many different methods and plans, but whatever the method or plan, CHRIST must be the message. *Reaping with Romans* is simply another method; one which I'm convinced, however, will enable anyone to fulfill the commission of the Lord.

Questions:

1. What is The Great Commission?

2. Who is a disciple of Christ?

3. How can you "make disciples?"

4. Everyone has a story. If you are comfortable to do so, please share your story.

A PHONE CALL—AN OPEN DOOR

While working with the Central Church in Davenport, Iowa, in 1973, a young lady called one afternoon and asked, "Do you study the Bible with people who aren't members of your church?"

"Yes, we do!" I answered, happy I didn't have to admit how seldom we studied the Bible with non-members! She then posed this question, "Can you come to our house at 8 o'clock tonight to study with my husband and me?" She added, "The Jehovah's Witnesses will be here at 6:30 p.m., and I don't want to start a fuss!"

I asked another member to go with me to Bob and Jo's home; we arrived promptly at 8 p.m. Even though the Jehovah's Witnesses were still there, we decided to go on in. After about 30 minutes the Witnesses left. We then engaged Bob and Jo in a Bible study.

Our objective was simple: to share Jesus Christ and him crucified. We opened to Romans 4 and began. Jesus was the essence of the study, not Bob and Jo, or anything else. We emphasized the provisions God has made for all of us—not the sinner and his obligation to God.

I asked them, "How will you respond to God who has given his Son for your salvation?"

Bob asked "What do I need to do?"

He went on to say that he often listened to television and radio preachers who pleaded, "Accept Christ as your Lord and Savior!" but never explained to Bob *how* he was to do that. He asked me, "Can you tell me what I need to do?"

I showed him Acts 2:36-38 where this very question was answered by Peter. *"Therefore let all Israel be assured of this: God has made this Jesus, whom you crucified, both Lord and Christ. When the people heard this, they were cut to the heart and said to Peter and the other apostles, 'Brothers, what shall we do?' Peter replied, Repent and be baptized, every one of you, in the name of Jesus Christ for the forgiveness of your sins. And you will receive the gift of the Holy Spirit.'"*

Bob and Jo immediately exclaimed, "This is what we want to do!"

That very night both were baptized into Jesus Christ (Galatians 3:27).

Bob said afterward, "Now, I'm not joining your church!" To which I replied, "I'm not asking you to join our church, I am simply assisting you as you follow the LORD." I knew that in surrendering his life to the Lord that Bob would join himself to a body of believers. Bob has been an active member of Central Church since his conversion. Today, almost 40 years later, Bob teaches the Junior High class, leading youngsters to define and deepen their faith in the Lord.

CHAPTER 4

WHERE DO I FIND OPEN HEARTS FOR THE MESSAGE?

Devote yourselves to prayer, being watchful and thankful. And pray for us, too, that God may open a door for our message, so that we may proclaim the mystery of Christ, for which I am in chains. Pray that I may proclaim it clearly, as I should. (Colossians 4:2-4)

Prayer is a very important component to saving the lost. This is more than just a quick mini type prayer. Paul says, *"Devote yourselves to prayer..."* Pray that you *"may proclaim the mystery of Christ."*

In Acts 16 there is an example of God intervening in the lives of a lady named Lydia and her companions:

> *On the Sabbath we went outside the city gate to the river, where we expected to find a place of prayer. We sat down and began to speak to the women who had gathered there. One of those listening was a woman named Lydia, a dealer in purple cloth from the city of Thyatira, who was a worshiper of God. The Lord opened her heart to respond to Paul's message.*

"The Lord opened her heart to respond..." Lydia was a worshiper of God so she was undoubtedly a person of prayer. It seems that Paul and company took them into their prayer meeting and Paul shared the message of salvation in Christ with the group. Prayer definitely played a part in Lydia coming to Christ.

During his ministry Christ was often surrounded by huge crowds. During one of these times he said to his disciples in Matthew 9:37-39:

"The harvest is plentiful but the workers are few. Ask the Lord of the harvest, therefore, to send out workers into his harvest field."

God instructs his disciples to ask God to send workers into the "harvest field." Pray. Pray that God will send forth workers to share the gospel with those that are outside of Christ.

It is when a person first comes to Christ that they are most likely to know of more opportunities to share Christ than at any other time in their Christian walk. Start with your family and friends. In informal survey after survey that I have done with groups it has been shown that over 90% of the people who come to Christ come as the result of a family member or a close friend

So, how do we get started?

TURNING THE CONVERSATION

If you were given an opportunity to share the gospel, what would you use to make a case for Christ? You need to have a plan, a method, and a message. This simple acrostic is very helpful to me:

F—Ask about their *Family. Listen.*

O—Ask about their *Occupation. Listen.*

R—Ask about their *Religion. Listen.*

M—Share the *Message. Talk.*

This simply gives you a track to run on and assumes that Christians approach people with the love of God. This is not meant to manipulate or trick. When you read the account of Jesus as he talked to the Samaritan woman at the well in John 4 you can see that he had a plan. Notice:

- He first got her attention (verses 7-9)

- He then got her interest (verses (10-12)

- Next he created a desire (verses 13-15)

- Then he caused conviction (verses 16-18)

- Finally, Jesus spoke to her as the Messiah (verses 19-26)

An effective way to turn a general conversation to spiritual matters is to ask, "Larry, may I ask you a personal question?" If he agrees you can do so, and then ask "How is your walk with the Lord?"

Another question to engage someone in a spiritual discussion is: "Have you reached a point in your relationship with God that you know you're going to heaven when you die?" If he is not certain about this question, then continue with, "Larry, I'd love to show you from God's word that you *can* know for sure whether you'd go to heaven. Did you know that a study in the book of Romans will reveal exactly how God feels about you, and the amazing gift he longs to give you?"

Or you could use the question my friend David Grubb has used effectively, "If I could show you a way from the Bible that you could stand before God without guilt and fear, would you be interested?"

A number of references in Scripture and my own personal experiences convince me that there is such a thing as "Divine Encounters." That is, God brings us into contact with people for the express purpose of our sharing the good news of Jesus. While on a door-knocking campaign in Iowa, a brother knocked on a door and the lady inside said, "Come in! I have been expecting you." The lady was blind and in a wheel chair. She explained a neighbor had been regularly reading the Bible to her, and she had decided several days before to commit her life to the Lord and be baptized. She said, "I know that God sent you!"

Consider the following Biblical example of Cornelius and his household in Acts 10. Cornelius was confronted by an "angel of God," while the Apostle Peter was seeing a vision on a rooftop where he had gone for prayer. All of this was instigated by God to bring these men together so Cornelius and his household could be saved. Cornelius had been told by the angel:

> "'Send to Joppa for Simon who is called Peter. He will bring you a message through which you and all your household will be saved.'" (Acts 11:13-14)

As you pray for opportunities to share Christ with others, expect Divine Encounters to take place.

David Grubb's Testimony

(David and Beverly Grubb were members of the
Central Church in Davenport, IA in 1973)

"It has been my experience that almost every time I have found a person interested in knowing and doing God's will, the Roman's Approach has met every need and been successful. Since I first started using it in Davenport in 1973, it has been my personal work study track for 40 years. (He set his GPS!)

When we came to Davenport, my wife and I were lifelong members of the church, and the fourth generation in both our families. Even so, we had no idea how to win souls and teach people the way of salvation. The Romans Approach study opened my eyes to credited righteousness and grace. Two things I knew nothing about before then. I believe that Romans 8:1-4 changed my entire view of God's will in our lives. I still use the basic study of Romans 4-8, Acts 2 & 8, and Luke 14. My only stumbling block over the years was starting in Romans 4:4-5 cold. To ease that block after getting to know people with the F-O-R-M approach, I have gone to Luke 23:32-43, referencing the man dying to sin. Then the transition question, "If I could show you a way from the Bible that you could stand before God without guilt and fear, would you be interested?" It has been my experience that the Roman's Approach shows the way.

I continue to use it and recommend that my students use it when they want to lead others to Christ. With this approach I always feel well equipped for any study challenge that comes my way."

David Grubb, Minister, Terre Haute, Ind.

Questions:

1. How do you get started in sharing Christ with others?

2. Examine Acts 10 and 11. Describe the "Divine Encounters" you see in these chapters.

3. What does it mean to *Devote* yourself to prayer?

4. Have you personally experienced a Divine Encounter?

Notes

SECTION II

Notes

A PLAN

We need a plan to present the gospel. The Romans Approach is a plan that you can put in your tool kit. After you have acquainted yourself with the study all you will need to proceed is a Bible. Following are some of the reasons this study is so effective:

1. The gospel is presented directly from the text. The gospel is the power that brings a person to Christ (Romans 1:16), not the presenter (2 Corinthians 4:7).

2. You can mark your Bible and easily follow the flow of Scripture as you share. I believe this to be the ideal way to present the gospel from Romans; however, I know of more than one situation where a person presented directly from the outline located at the end of this book. Yes, some accepted Christ as a result of that approach. Use this outline to mark your Bibles before you begin, make marginal notes in your Bible, and present the study to another Christian as a practice run.

3. Engage the person in dialogue as you study. Let them ask questions that are in the text you are dealing with. For questions not related to the text, write them down with a promise to discuss them later.

4. It is transferable, so the person with whom you share can not only comprehend what you have presented, but can easily share this study with others.

5. You can present the gospel and bring a person to a decision for Christ in as little as one study. (This is not to say you should not have multiple studies with a person who has the desire to become a Christian.)

6. You may judge yourself clumsy as you initially present the gospel from Romans, but go ahead anyway. Experience can only be gained by actually doing it.

CHAPTER 5

✹ —————— ✹

SHARING THE GOSPEL FROM ROMANS THE ROMANS APPROACH

I am not ashamed of the gospel, because it is the power of God for the salvation of everyone who believes: first for the Jew, then for the Gentile. For in the gospel a righteousness from God is revealed, a righteousness that is by faith from first to last, just as it is written: "The righteous will live by faith." (Romans 1:16-17)

Steve the Messenger

Steve and Teresa were new Christians in our church family. I had shared the gospel from Romans with both of them and rejoiced with them when they acted on their decision to become Christians. Almost from the beginning Steve was eager to tell others about finding God.

My practice was to take a new Christian along with me to watch and learn as I presented the gospel message to others; after several studies, I invited the babe in Christ to take the lead. Once Steve had gone with me a few times, I judged him ready to share on his own. He agreed excitedly to do so. At my next appointment, we sat down with the couple, opened our Bibles and Steve began. I sat back, expecting my protégé to do me proud.

I began to lose my laid-back feeling very quickly. In fact after only a very few minutes, my insides were in a nervous knot. I wanted to put my head in my hands, but refrained. I tried to look pleasant as I thought, "The gospel is far too important to let him butcher it this way!!"

However, for whatever reason, I did not interrupt. He continued bumbling along, awkwardly saying things at the wrong time (by my estimation), and leaving out things he should have said (in my way of thinking). Toward the end of the study I sighed, sure he had blown a golden opportunity to bring this couple to Christ.

Little did I know! Steve finally asked, "Do you believe that Jesus Christ is the Son of God?" Both these precious people said, "Yes!" Just like with the Ethiopian in Acts 8, they were baptized into Jesus Christ that same day.

Truly, the gospel is the power of God for salvation (Romans 1:16). The power is embodied in the message, not in the messenger, nor in the presentation of the message.

ROMANS 4
THE MESSAGE

This study begins in Romans 4:1 and goes through Romans 8:1. I tell people, "I treat this study as I would a ripe watermelon in Arkansas during the peak of the watermelon growing season. You go to the watermelon field, pick a melon, and drop it on the ground to burst it open, then reach in and take the heart out of it." So, like with the watermelon, instead of reading every verse, we'll extract the heart out of this letter to the Romans.

As we begin, read Romans 4:1-3:

> *"What then shall we say that Abraham, our forefather, discovered in this matter? If, in fact, Abraham was justified by works, he had something to boast about—but not before God." What does the Scripture say? "Abraham believed God, and it was credited to him as righteousness."*

I read this many times as, "Abraham believed *in* God . . . " but that's incorrect. The Holy Spirit says specifically that Abraham BELIEVED God. When God spoke, Abraham obeyed.

Notice what God said to Abraham in Genesis 12:1-3 as he blessed him with the promise:

> *"Leave your country, your people and your father's household and go to the land I will show you. I will make you into a great nation and I will bless you; I will bless those who bless you, and whoever curses you I will curse; and all peoples on earth will be blessed through you. So Abram departed . . . "*

Did you notice just three words are used to describe his response? **"So Abram departed . . ."** Abraham was in relationship with God. Paul uses Abraham to show us the basis of man's relationship to God. When God spoke Abraham believed what God said and acted on it.

Read Romans 4:4-5:

> *"Now when a man works, his wages are not credited to him as a gift, but as an obligation. However, to the man who does not work but trusts God who justifies the wicked, his faith is credited as righteousness."*

Man's relationship with God is not merited by works, but rather is offered as a gift. If I promise to pay you $50 for a day's work and you complete the day's job and receive $50, have I given you a gift? Certainly not. You've received what you've earned. I simply paid you the debt I owed you.

On the other hand, suppose someone offers you a trillion dollars—more money than anyone could earn or spend in a lifetime. That's enough to dam up the Mississippi River at the Gulf. With a trillion dollars you could line up $100 dollar bills end-to-end and circle the globe several times. A trillion dollars is simply beyond our earning capacity! We cannot *do* anything to merit that amount of money. If we ever have a trillion dollars, it will be because someone gives it to us.

Let's say someone presents us a certified check for $1,000,000,000,000. We're instructed to simply sign our name in the blank that says, "Pay to the Order of," deposit it into our bank account, and it's ours! Have we earned it? Of course not. We've merely accepted it. You cannot earn what is impossible to earn.

Salvation, like a trillion dollars, is unearnable and undeservable. No one can ever be worthy of salvation, or do a work great enough to warrant it. Surely no one would demand that he be made right with God by the Savior's sacrifice on the cross because he somehow has earned it.

We must be willing to accept wholeheartedly—without doubting—that Jesus died for our sins and desires that we be righteous in his sight. As it is said of Abraham, our example, in Romans 4:20-24:

> *"Yet he did not waver through unbelief regarding the promise of God, but was strengthened in his faith and gave glory to God, being fully persuaded that God had power to do what he had promised. This is why 'it was credited to him as righteousness'" (verses 20-22).*

Notice the verses that follow:

> *"The words 'it was credited to him' were written not for him alone, but also for us, to whom God will credit righteousness—for us who believe in him who raised Jesus our Lord from the dead" (verses 23-24).*

The words, "It was credited to him" (or imputed or reckoned) were not written just for Abraham, but for US also. God will do for us what he did for Abraham IF we do what Abraham did; that is, believe God.

Romans 4:25 states:

> *"He was delivered over to death for our sins and was raised to life for our justification."*

It is a fact that Jesus lived, died, and was buried. It's also a fact that he left that tomb on the third day. He rose up from the dead! Jesus died and was raised to life for our sins, and also for our justification. To be justified is to stand before God cleansed of wrong doing. It is, "Just-as-if-I'd-never-sinned."

Questions:

1.   Calculate how long it would take to make a Trillion Dollars earning $10 per hour. Could you ever earn a Trillion Dollars?

2.   Can salvation be earned? If so, how?

3.   How was Abraham made righteous?

4.   What does it mean to "waver through unbelief?"

5.   Who were the words, "it was credited to him," written for?

CHAPTER 6

But now a righteousness from God, apart from law, has been made known, to which the Law and the Prophets testify. (Romans 3:21)

ROMANS 5

When we fully trust God for our salvation, we will be at peace with him. As Romans 5:1 tells us:

> *"Therefore, since we have been justified through faith, we have peace with God through our Lord Jesus Christ . . . "*

Peace is the opposite of war. Peace means the war is over. The conflict is resolved. We can now have harmony, tranquility and joy, knowing that God through His gift of Jesus Christ will credit us with righteousness.

Salvation is divinely *credited* through Christ. Unfortunately, some people do not have this peace because they focus on themselves and their ability to merit salvation by good works. Those who do not have peace place the emphasis on the sinner, and the sinner's obligation to God. Where does God place the emphasis? He magnifies Christ and the provision of salvation through him.

Romans 5:8-10:

> "But God demonstrates his own love for us in this: While we were still sinners, **Christ died for us**. Since we have now been **justified by his blood**, how much more shall we be **saved from God's wrath through him**! For if, when we were God's enemies, we were **reconciled to him through the death of his Son**, how much more, having been reconciled, shall we be **saved through his life!**"

Notice: *"Christ died for us," "justified by his blood," "saved from God's wrath through him," "reconciled to him through the death of his Son," and "saved through his life."* Where is the emphasis? Clearly on <u>Christ</u> and the provision of salvation he offers.

We are saved, not by our lives, but by HIS LIFE. The righteousness of Christ is *applied to our account* if we are willing to receive it.

Consider this story about an orphan lamb, and a shepherd who was very attached to the lamb. Because he wanted his cherished pet to live, he tried to get a ewe sheep with a lamb of her own to accept the orphan. She rejected it. After all methods failed, the shepherd slaughtered the ewe sheep's own little innocent lamb, removed its hide, and draped it over his pet lamb. When he took it to the ewe this time, she smelled the familiar scent of her own offspring and accepted the orphan lamb as her own.

You may be thinking, "I don't like that story! That's not fair!" Nevertheless, that's what God has done for us. He loved us so dearly he allowed his own Son to die for our sins, then, upon our acceptance of him as the Son of God he clothed us with the Son's righteousness so he could accept us as his own offspring. God *cannot* accept us on the basis of our human righteousness (Isaiah 64:6), but welcomes us if we're clothed in the righteousness of Christ. Jesus Christ's righteousness makes *us* right with God (2 Corinthians. 5:21).

Now notice the lesson from Romans 5:12:

> *"Therefore, just as sin entered the world through one man, and death through sin, and in this way death came to all men, because all sinned . . . "*

All includes you and me. *All* means everyone. Who is the "one man" mentioned here? Answer: Adam.

Notice now Romans 5:13-14:

> *"For before the law was given, sin was in the world. But sin is not taken into account when there is no law. Nevertheless, death reigned from the time of Adam to the time of Moses, even over those who did not sin by*

breaking a command, as did Adam, who was a pattern of the one to come."

What was the first law given to mankind? Answer: *"You must not eat from the tree of the knowledge of good and evil . . . "* (Genesis 2:17). What was the next law given by God? Answer: The Law of Moses on Sinai. If the people who lived before Moses were not under any law, why did they die? Answer: As a consequence of Adam's sin.

To illustrate this, let's say I get into a game of gambling. I think I have a good chance to win, and bet high, but I lose—big time: next year's salary, my house, and car—all my possessions. Who has sinned? Answer: I have. But who will *also* suffer? Answer: My entire family.

We did not disobey God by eating the forbidden fruit, BUT . . . we do suffer the *consequence* of Adam's sin because we're members of Adam's family. Verse 14 says that Adam was a pattern of the Christ who was to come. Yes, we die as a consequence of Adam's sin, but the good news is that we may *live* as a result of the righteousness of the Lamb of God, Jesus Christ!

GOD HAS A GIFT FOR YOU

This righteousness of Christ is a gift; one which God desires to give each of us through Jesus, his son. As you read this passage, notice how many times the word "gift" is used in Romans 5:15-18:

"But the gift is not like the trespass. For if the many died by the trespass of the one man, how much more did God's grace and the gift that came by the grace of the one man, Jesus Christ, overflow to the many! Again, the gift of God is not like the result of the one man's sin: The judgment followed one sin and brought condemnation, but the gift followed many trespasses and brought justification. For if, by the trespass of the one man, death reigned through that one man, how much more will those who receive God's abundant provision of grace and of the gift of righteousness reign in life through the one man, Jesus Christ. Consequently, just as the result of one trespass was condemnation for all men, so also the result of one act of righteousness was justification that brings life for all men:"

Why is the word, "gift" used so many times in this short reading? God wants us to know that salvation is a gift! You cannot earn a gift; you can only accept it or reject it.

Once when my wife and I were visiting in the home of dear friends, I asked the lady of the house to go through the Romans Approach with us after dinner. Gail was an intelligent, devoted Christian, and I not only wanted to share the message of Romans with her, but also wanted her assessment of the study. When we got to Romans 5:15-18—when she realized the full impact of the word "gift," she was quiet for a very long moment, just looking at me. Then she softly said, almost with shock, "Jim, that's too good to be true!" I replied, "Now you're catching on!"

The gift is not like the trespass: To underscore this reality, Adam is compared to Christ: As a consequence of Adam's sin, death entered the world and we will all die. But the gift of Christ is *not* like the sin of that first man. Adam was a sinner; Christ was absolutely righteous. While Adam's sin led to death, the righteousness of Christ offers eternal life—a great contrast! Adam brought death; Christ brings eternal life. We didn't choose to be born as human beings; however, we *can* choose to make Jesus Christ the Lord of our lives. Notice the following comparison:

"But the gift is not like the trespass."

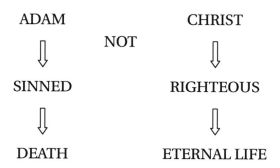

59

Adam's sin brought death; the righteousness of Christ brings
eternal life. Romans 5:18-19 sums up the contrast between
Adam and Christ by saying:

> *"Consequently, just as the result of one trespass was
> condemnation for all men, so also the result of one act
> of righteousness was justification that brings life for
> all men. For just as through disobedience of the one
> man the many were made sinners, so also through
> the obedience of the one man many will be made
> righteous."*

Adam committed the one trespass.

Christ provided the one act of righteousness.

Adam's disobedience made many sinners.

Christ's obedience will make many righteous.

Romans 5:20 further explains:

> *"Where sin increased, grace increased all the more . . . "*

Sin cannot overpower God's grace.

You might conclude at this point that since salvation is totally dependent upon Christ, because his righteousness makes me righteous, I will accept his righteousness, receive the gift, and live just as I please! "I'll sin and let grace cover it!"

Only one problem with this conclusion: IT WON'T WORK!

Questions:

1. What does it mean to have peace with God?

2. Where does God place the focus in Romans 5 on the sinner and the sinner's obligation to Himself, or on Christ and His provision of salvation? Romans 5:8-10

3. Can a gift be earned?

4. Is God's grace sufficient to cover all sins?

5. Explain how Christ's "one act of righteousness" is capable of covering all sins.

CHAPTER 7

God presented him as a sacrifice of atonement, through faith in his blood. He did this to demonstrate his justice . . . at the present time, so as to be just and the one who justifies those who have faith in Jesus. (Romans 3:25a-26b)

ROMANS 6

Can we deliberately choose to sin and expect grace to cover us? Paul begins to answer this question in the opening verses of Romans 6:1-4:

"What shall we say, then? Shall we go on sinning so that grace may increase? By no means! We died to sin; how can we live in it any longer? Or don't you know that all of us who were baptized into Christ Jesus were baptized into his death?" (Question: What do you do with a a person who has died?) "We were therefore buried with him through baptism into death in order that, just as Christ was raised from the dead through the glory of the Father, we too may live a new life."

In verses 12-16 Paul continues to combat the idea that a person can serve sin and be righteous. Look at the key word in this section, which is *offer* (means to *yield*):

"Therefore do not let sin reign in your mortal body so that you obey its evil desires. Do not offer the parts of your body to sin, as instruments of wickedness, but rather offer yourselves to God, as those who have been brought from death to life; and offer the parts of your body to him as instruments of righteousness."

To sum up, Don't let sin be your ruler. Do not let it conquer you.

The key word *offer* is translated *yield* in other versions of the Bible. It's a word used to describe what happened in a wrestling match when an opponent gave up to his competitor. When a wrestler stopped trying to keep a shoulder raised off the mat, he had offered himself or *yielded* to his opponent. When we give in to sin, we have yielded to it. As long as we're resisting (fighting back) we have not surrendered.

Notice, the text is clear that we are to offer ourselves to God, and refuse to offer ourselves to sin. If a person sins deliberately, expecting grace to increase accordingly to cover him, he is deceiving himself. He has instead become a *servant of sin*—and spiritual death will be the result. However, if one continually yields to righteousness, offers himself to righteous living, God's overflowing grace will cover any sins he does commit.

Paul wrote of the Roman Christians in 6:17-18:

> *But thanks be to God, that, though you used to be slaves to sin, you wholeheartedly obeyed the form of teaching to which you were entrusted. You have been set free from sin and have become slaves to righteousness.*

When were the Romans set free from sin? Answer: When they wholeheartedly obeyed the form of teaching.

To wholeheartedly obey means more than superficially obeying; it's more than just going through a ritual or submitting to a church rule. It means to completely give oneself to the Lord. Notice what they did: with all their hearts they had submitted to the form of teaching Paul had shared with them. When they surrendered their hearts in obedience they were made free from sin. They actually changed from serving their flesh to serving Jesus as Lord.

Paul's message from this section is summed up in Romans 6:23:

> *For the wages of sin is death, but the gift of God is eternal life in Christ Jesus our Lord.*

The only way your sin-debt will ever be paid is through Jesus Christ. You can't pay your sin-debt even by going to hell because hell is eternal. If you go there, it would be *forever* (Matthew 25:46; Revelation 20:10, 14). What a price Christ paid for our redemption!

Notice, the wages of sin is death. The **FREE GIFT** of God is eternal life. You cannot earn a gift; you can only accept it or reject it.

Questions:

1.   Why can't we just sin and let God's grace cover it?

2.   What does it mean to *die to sin*?

3.   What does it mean to *offer* your members to sin?

4.   What does it mean to *offer* your members to God?

5.   How can our sin-debt be paid?

6.   Can you earn a gift? Is salvation a gift?

CHAPTER 8

Where, then, is boasting? It is excluded. On what principle? On that of observing the law? No, but on that of faith. For we maintain that a man is justified by faith apart from observing the law. (Romans 3:27-28)

ROMANS 7

In Romans 7: 14-19 Paul reveals the struggle between flesh and spirit:

> *"We know that the law is spiritual, but I am unspiritual, sold as a slave to sin. I do not understand what I do. For what I want to do I do not do, but what I hate I do. And if I do what I do not want to do, I agree that the law is good. As it is, it is no longer I myself who do it, but it is sin living in me. I know that nothing good lives in me, that is, in my sinful nature. For I have the desire to do what is good, but I cannot carry it out. For what I do is not the good I want to do; no, the evil I do not want to do—this I keep on doing. Now if I do what I do not want to do, it is no longer I who do it, but it is sin living in me that does it."*

Here Paul describes a tension that exists in every human being—a conflict in wanting to do right, but, at the same time, powerless on our own, to carry through with this desire. Paul experienced this helplessness: he longed to do what was right, but was unable to perform it. Frustrated at every turn, he recognized that nothing good lives in his flesh (sinful nature); he would never, in and of himself, be clever enough, competent enough, or intelligent enough to break free from sin's slavery. Neither will we! Where, and in whom, is there any way out of this unbearable dilemma? In verses 21-22 Paul concludes that though our spirits seek after God, our fleshly nature wants only to obey the law of sin. Our sinful natures crave to be slaves of sin.

Because of this realization Paul exclaims in verse 24:

> *"What a wretched man I am! WHO will rescue me from this body of death?"*

This resounding answer follows immediately:

> *"Thanks be to God—**through Jesus Christ our Lord!**"*

Christ is the answer!! Jesus gives us righteousness, and he gives us spiritual victory over our sinful natures—breaks the power of sin to enslave us. **Note:** To no longer be slaves to sin does not mean that Christians never sin (1 John 1:8). The good news is that Jesus gives us a *new nature* inhabited by the Holy Spirit who frees us from *slavery* to sin (Romans 6:17-18).

What are we to do when we mess up? Repent. My friend Gary Lambrecht used to say Christians live on "repentance road"—that is, in this life we never stop growing, never stop maturing, never stop moving nearer to the nature of Jesus. When we spot deficiencies in our lives—sins of omission or sins of commission, we repent.

We are all in this thing together—we all have proceeded from the first man, Adam. Because of that fact, we all have incurred a debt we cannot pay, since *everyone* is a sinner just as Adam was (Romans 3:23). In spite of this bad news, God has good news! He's made a way for sinners to be saved!

Here is how: I am a sinner and, consequently, have a sin-debt I can *never, ever* pay (Romans 3:10, 23). Jesus Christ paid a sin-debt he did not owe because he never sinned. (Hebrews. 4:15; 2 Corinthians 5:21). Since he paid a debt he didn't owe, and we have a debt we cannot pay, Jesus makes this offer: "If you will accept the debt I paid and didn't owe, I will cancel the debt you have to pay and cannot pay!"

In the last part of Romans 7:25 Paul concludes:

> *"So then, I myself in my mind am a slave to God's law,*
> *but in the sinful nature a slave to the law of sin."*

In this life we never stop growing, never stop maturing, never stop moving nearer to the nature of Jesus. When we spot deficiencies in our lives—sins of omission or sins of commission, we repent.

ROMANS 8

The Lord sums up what our relationship to his Son can be by saying in Romans 8:1, 4:

> *"Therefore there is now no condemnation for those who are in Christ Jesus, because through Christ Jesus the law of the Spirit of life set me free from the law of sin and death . . . in order that the righteous requirements of the law might be fully met in us, who do not live according to the sinful nature but according to the Spirit."*

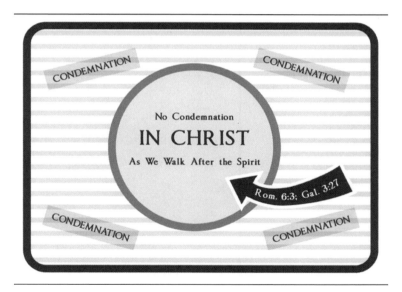

There is *right now* no condemnation to those who are "in Christ Jesus" and "living according to the Spirit." To live according to the Spirit means yielding to righteousness. One who yields to righteousness accepts the teachings of God's word, and is steadily conforming his life to God's purposes.

Question: Are you yielding to righteousness? You are if you are submitting to Jesus as Lord of your life.

You must also be *in Jesus Christ.* How does one get *into* Christ? Let's look again at Romans 6:3:

> *Don't you know that all of us who were baptized **into** Christ Jesus were baptized into his death?*

Also Galatians 3:27 says:

> *For all of you who were baptized **into** Christ have clothed yourselves with Christ.*

It really is all about Jesus!

Questions:

1. Can you describe the tension Paul speaks of in Romans 7:14-19?

2.   Why couldn't the law deliver Paul from this tension?

3.   Who could deliver Paul from his wretchedness?

4.   What does it mean to be "in Christ?"

5.   What does it mean to "walk after the Spirit?"

CHAPTER 9

✵ ———•— ✦

For it is by grace you have been saved, through faith—and this not from yourselves, it is the gift of God—not by works, so that no one can boast. (Ephesians 2:8-9)

A SUMMARY

Here is a quick summary of what we have covered: All our self-righteous deeds are like filthy rags before God (Isaiah 64:6). Paul declared that *"There is no one righteous, not even one . . . "* (Romans 3:10), so God sent his one and only Son, who never sinned, to become our "righteousness." 2 Corinthians 5:21 states this fact, *"God made him who had no sin to be sin for us, so that in him we might become the righteousness of God."* In the first letter to the Corinthians Paul wrote:

> *"It is because of him that you are in Christ Jesus, who has become for us wisdom from God—that is, our righteousness, holiness and redemption. Therefore, as it is written: 'Let him who boasts boast in the Lord.'" (1 Corinthians 1:30-31).*

These truths emphasize how important it is for you to accept the gift of salvation by being "baptized into Christ" and consequently, being "clothed" with Christ's righteousness.

Barry & Nancy's Story

Jim and Tony, who were twins, had recently become Christians. They worked for Barry, district supervisor for a national insurance company. The three often traveled together, giving Jim and Tony many occasions to discuss the gospel with their boss. They learned he had never fully given his life to the Lord.

Jim and Tony contacted me, and asked if I would set up a Bible study with their supervisor and his wife, Nancy. They soon introduced me to Barry. I asked him to give me a call when they were ready to study, though I really didn't expect to hear back from him!

Barry did call and asked that I come to their home on a Saturday morning for Bible study with him and his wife, Nancy. We sat down around their dining table and opened our Bibles. After prayer I asked if I could pose a personal question—they agreed. I asked, "Have you reached a place in your spiritual life where you know for sure that if you died today you would go to heaven?" They both answered that they had, and we began our study of Romans.

At the conclusion, we read Romans 8:1, *"Therefore, there is now no condemnation for those who are in Christ Jesus."* I immediately asked, "Are you in Christ?" They replied that they were.

"How did you get into Christ?" I further inquired.

"We invited him into our hearts."

I then pointed out, "That may be how *Christ* got into *you*, but this scripture specifically says there's no condemnation for those who are *IN Christ*. We need to see what Scripture says about getting *into Christ*.

We had earlier read Romans 6:3-4:

> *Or don't you know that all of us who were baptized into Christ Jesus were baptized into his death? We were therefore buried with him through baptism into death in order that, just as Christ was raised from the dead through the glory of the Father, we too may live a new life.*

I asked, "Have either of you ever been buried with Christ in baptism?" Nancy quickly processed what her answer would mean, and fled to her bedroom, weeping. She had never been immersed with Christ.

Barry and I were silent for a time. Finally I asked him, "What are you going to do?"

He shook his head, "Jim I'm just not ready to receive baptism!"

"Barry, I did *not* come over here to get you to receive baptism. I came over to share *Jesus* with you. You aren't saying no to baptism, you are saying no to Christ!"

Barry responded, "Boy, it's not hard to say no to baptism, but it sure is difficult to say no to Christ!"

This was another point of enlightenment for me. Baptism is not a person. You cannot have an ongoing relationship with baptism. Baptism is a *what*. Jesus Christ, the Son of God, is a *Person*. You can have a relationship with him. He is a *Who*.

Barry and Nancy were both baptized into the Lord.

PITFALLS TO AVOID

As you teach the gospel using Romans you must avoid at least two things. First, don't get bogged down on baptism when you get to Romans 6:2, You ask, "What do we do with someone who has died?" The answer is: "You bury them." Without making a comment, read verses 3 and 4, then proceed on to verse 12, continuing the study.

Secondly, do not shift from the scriptural emphasis of "Who" to the unscriptural emphasis of "what." Paul says in Romans 7:24—*"Who will rescue me from this body of death?"* Not *what* would rescue him, but *Who*. Paul trusted in *Someone* rather than *some thing*.

He later wrote Timothy that: *"God . . . has saved us and called us to a holy life—not because of anything we have done but because of his own purpose and grace"* (2 Timothy. 1:9).

He stated further in verse 12*: "I know <u>whom</u> I have believed and am convinced that <u>he</u> is able to guard what I have entrusted to <u>him</u> for that day."*

79

Jesus stressed changing the inner man. His rebuke to those with ungodly hearts was, *"First clean the inside of the cup and dish, and then the outside also will be clean" (Matthew 23:26).* If we convert individuals to *Who* saves us—Jesus Christ—they will be clean, inside and out! (1 John. 2:3-4)

It's dangerous to teach people WHAT the Bible commands—merely rule-keeping, and ignore *Who* saves us—Jesus Christ. The Pharisees appeared to be extremely religious by obsessively tithing, fasting, praying, making proselytes, and attending temple services. They knew the *what* of their religion, but rejected the *Who*—Jesus himself. (Matthew 15:8-9)

As you study with those who are outside Christ, keep the emphasis where God put it—on Jesus Christ. The question is, "What will you do with Jesus?"

CONVERSION EXAMPLES FROM ACTS

After sharing how to get into Christ, you can then look at examples in the book of Acts. In Acts 2 Peter preaches the same gospel taught in Romans. In verses 22-24, he proclaimed:

> *Men of Israel, listen to this: Jesus of Nazareth was a man accredited by God to you by miracles, wonders*

and signs, which God did among you through him, as you yourselves know. This man was handed over to you by God's set purpose and foreknowledge; and you, with the help of wicked men, put him to death by nailing him to the cross. But God raised him from the dead, freeing him from the agony of death, because it was impossible for death to keep its hold on him.

In verse 32 Peter focused on the reason the grave where they had laid Jesus was empty. He said:

God has raised this Jesus to life, and we are all witnesses of the fact.

He concluded by saying in verse 36:

Therefore, let all Israel be assured of this: God has made this Jesus, whom you crucified, both LORD and Christ.

Peter preached Jesus; his death, burial and resurrection.

How did the crowd respond? Acts 2:37 says:

"When the people heard this, they were cut to the heart and said to Peter and the other apostles, 'Brothers, what shall we do?'"

Peter's answer is in verse 38:

"Repent and be baptized, every one of you, in the name of Jesus Christ for the forgiveness of your sins. And you will receive the gift of the Holy Spirit."

Repentance is "dying to sin," while baptism is a burial of the person who has "died to sin." In the light of Romans 6, we could paraphrase Acts 2:38 in this way: *Die to sin, then bury the dead man of sin with Christ in baptism. Being then made free from sin, you receive the gift of God's Holy Spirit to live in you.*

Is this promise of God offered to us today?

"The promise is for you and your children and for all who are far off—for all whom the Lord our God will call" (Acts 2:39).

How did the crowd (to whom Peter was preaching) react to his instructions?

"Those who accepted his message were baptized, and about three thousand were added to their number that day. (Acts 2:41)

Who was the centerpiece of Peter's message? Since Jesus is the Message, who did this repentant crowd accept, and what followed?

"They devoted themselves to the apostles' teaching and to the fellowship, to the breaking of bread and to prayer." (Acts 2:42)

The idea of devoting themselves means they dedicated themselves to carefully follow all the apostles taught in word and deed. This group of believers, over 3000 strong, *"broke bread in their homes and ate together with glad and sincere hearts, praising God and enjoying the favor of all the people." (Acts 2:46)*

What will God do for you if you follow the example of the people in Acts 2? (Acts 2:39)

1. Forgive your sins.

2. Put you into Jesus Christ!

3. Give you the Holy Spirit.

4. Add you to his church.

What will you in turn find to be your responsibility? Dedicate yourself to:

1. The apostles' doctrine (the teachings of Scripture)

2. The fellowship of Christians, that is the breaking of bread

3. Prayer

Questions:

1. To whom did the lost wholeheartedly give themselves? Answer: Jesus Christ

2. Who added them to Jesus' church? Answer: God.

3. How many churches did the Lord add the lost to? Answer: The one church.

4. Whose church was it? Answer: Christ's.

5. Compare Peter's sermon in Acts 2 with the teachings of Paul from Romans.

CHAPTER 10

*That if you confess with your mouth, "Jesus is Lord,"
and believe in your heart that God raised him from the
dead, you will be saved. **10** For it is with your heart that
you believe and are justified, and it is with your mouth
that you confess and are saved. (Ephesians 2:8-9)*

A LOOK AT ACTS 8

The story that follows is what I refer to as a "Divine Encounter." This is a God arranged meeting between Philip, a Christian, and an Ethiopian eunuch, who is an unsaved seeker. The narrative begins in Acts 8:26:

"Now an angel of the Lord said to Philip, 'Go south to the road—the desert road—that goes down from Jerusalem to Gaza.' So he started out, and on his way he met an Ethiopian eunuch, an important official in charge of all the treasury of Candace, queen of the Ethiopians. This man had gone to Jerusalem to worship and on his way home was sitting in his chariot reading the book of Isaiah the prophet. The Spirit told Philip, 'Go to that chariot and stay near it.'

"Then Philip ran up to the chariot and heard the man reading Isaiah the prophet, 'Do you understand what you are reading?' Philip asked. 'How can I,' he said, 'unless someone explains it to me?' So he invited Philip to come up and sit with him. The eunuch was reading this passage of Scripture:

'He was led like a sheep to the slaughter, and as a lamb before the shearer is silent, so he did not open his mouth. In his humiliation he was deprived of justice. Who can

speak of his descendants? For his life was taken from the earth'" (Isaiah 53:7-8).

This prophecy of the coming Messiah confused the Ethiopian official, who followed the Law of Moses. Notice Verses 34-35:

The eunuch asked Philip, "Tell me, please, who is the prophet talking about, himself or someone else?" Then Philip began with that very passage of Scripture and told him the good news about Jesus.

How did the eunuch react to Philip's teaching?

"Look, here is water. Why shouldn't I be baptized?" (Vs. 36)

Philip had, in the words of Scripture, *told him the good news about Jesus,* so why did the eunuch ask to be baptized? And what was Philip's reply as recorded in some of the later manuscripts of Acts?

"If you believe with all your heart, you may" (2:37). Wholehearted obedience!

The official responded as recorded in a footnote of most
Bibles:

> *"I believe that Jesus Christ is the Son of God . . . Then*
> *both Philip and the eunuch went down into the water*
> *and Philip baptized him. When they came up out of*
> *the water, the Spirit of the Lord suddenly took Philip*
> *away, and the eunuch did not see him again, but went*
> *on his way rejoicing" (Vs. 37-39).*

Question: Why did both men go down into the water? Answer:
So the eunuch could be buried.

Question: Why was the eunuch rejoicing as he continued his
journey? Answer: His sins were forgiven; he had believed in
Jesus and he had obeyed from the heart!

A LOOK AT DISCIPLESHIP

Do not baptize anyone who is not ready to be a disciple of Christ. The instructions handed down through the apostles (Matthew 28:19-20) to Christians today are to make disciples by baptizing them and then teaching them, to observe all that God has commanded. Disciples are followers of Jesus Christ. God first wants our hearts.

Paul's statement in 1 Corinthians 1:17 should resonate with every Christian working to win the lost:

"For Christ did not send me to baptize, but to preach the gospel."

In Matthew 28:19 we read:

"Therefore go and make disciples of all nations, baptizing them in the name of the Father and of the Son and of the Holy Spirit . . . "

Only those willing to surrender their lives to God should be baptized. Note this emphasis on discipleship in Luke 14:15-35:

1. Jesus, in speaking of those who will eat at the feast in God's kingdom, illustrates with a story of a banquet prepared for certain invited guests—the Jews. (vs. 15-17)

2. However, these would-be guests began to make excuses. (vs. 18-20)

   - "I have just bought a field . . . "

   - "I have just bought five yoke of oxen . . . "

   - "I just got married . . . "

3. Because the Jews rejected God's invitation, he invited the Gentiles to come to the feast. (vs. 23)

4. The Lord barred from his banquet every person who used an excuse to stay away. (vs. 24)

5. In verse 26 Jesus rebuked excuse-making instead of accepting and following him:

   "If anyone comes to me and does not hate his father and mother, his wife and children, his brothers and sisters—yes, even his own life—he cannot be my disciple."

   - Note that unless a person loves Jesus Christ more than anybody else, that individual cannot be a disciple of Jesus.

- What if a loved one tries to hinder us from obeying Christ? Will we love and honor Jesus above everyone else? We may still retain our family, homes, etc. but we must surrender ownership and control of them to Jesus.

6. Not only can other people stand in the way of our giving all to Jesus; possessions can ensnare us too! In Luke 14, 27 and 33, the Lord declares:

   "Anyone who does not carry his cross and follow me cannot be my disciple ... Any of you who does not give up everything he has cannot be my disciple."

- If it were the Lord's will that you leave your home, relatives, friends, the security of your job and retirement benefits, would you do it? If not, would you still be his disciple?

7. Count the cost and be willing to pay the price. (Luke. 14:28-32)

Again, *"There is no condemnation for those that are in Christ ... walking after the Spirit" (Romans 8:1,4).*

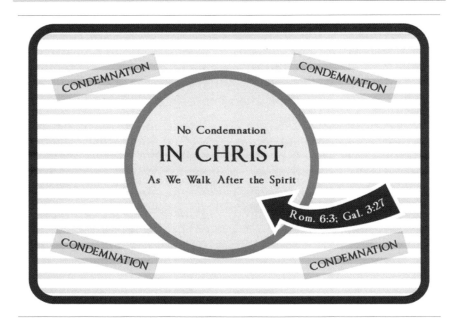

Are you in Christ walking after the Spirit?

Questions:

1. Was the Ethiopian lost or saved when God sent Philip to him?

2. What did Philip preach to the eunuch? What was the eunuch's response?

3. Why did this man desire to be baptized?

4. In what ways is the conversion of the Ethiopian similar to Acts 2 and Romans 4-8?

5. What does it mean to walk after the Spirit?

CHAPTER 11

Was not our ancestor Abraham considered righteous for what he did when he offered his son Isaac on the altar? You see that his faith and his actions were working together, and his faith was made complete by what he did. And the scripture was fulfilled that says, "Abraham believed God, and it was credited to him as righteousness," and he was called God's friend. (James 2:21-23)

ABRAHAM, OUR EXAMPLE

Abraham is included in the Romans study because he is an example of one made righteous by faith. According to Romans 4: 9-10, God gave righteousness to Abraham *before* he was circumcised, and *before* God gave the law to the Israelites. Therefore, righteousness was given to him because of his faith—not because of his works.

In Genesis 12:1-3 God blessed Abraham with this promise:

> *"Leave your country, your people and your father's household and go to the land I will show you. I will make you into a great nation and I will bless you; I will bless those who bless you, and whoever curses you I will curse; and all peoples on earth will be blessed through you."*

God justified Abraham when he was 75 years old—before he was circumcised (Genesis. 12:4). In fact, the Lord didn't institute circumcision as the sign of his covenant with Abraham until 24 years later, when he was 99. In addition, Mosaic Law didn't come into being until 430 years *after* Abraham had been made right with God by his faith (Galatians 3:16-18). Thus, Abraham was saved previous to God's commandment that circumcision be a sign for their covenant; he stood righteous in God's sight before circumcision became a sign of the agreement between

God and with his chosen people—even before he offered Isaac as a sacrifice! (Genesis. 22:1-13)

When God spoke, Abraham believed what he said and acted. He is an example of one made righteous by faith! His life models the kind of faith we must possess to be justified. Abraham recognized the God *"Who gives life to the dead, and calls things that are not as though they were" (Romans 4:17).* We Christians must also have this kind of faith (Romans 10:9-10).

"Against all hope, Abraham in hope believed" (Rom. 4:18). He was 100 years old and Sarah was 90 when God announced to them they would have a son—a biological son! (Genesis 17:15-17). Abraham's reaction? He fell to the ground and laughed! Sarah laughed too, later, when she heard that same promise. Although they were well beyond child-bearing ability, Abraham and Sarah chose to believe God in spite of the obvious physical facts:

"Without weakening in his faith, he faced the fact that his body was as good as dead—since he was about a hundred years old—and that Sarah's womb was also dead" (Romans 4:19).

And consider this from Romans 4:20:

"He did not waver through unbelief regarding the promise of God, but was strengthened in his faith and gave glory to God, being fully persuaded that God had power to do what he had promised."

If that doesn't illustrate unfaltering, unswerving faith, nothing does! Abraham believed God even when God asked him to do the unbelievable.

Abraham's faith enabled him to claim God's promise, and through faith, God credited him with righteousness (Romans 4:22).

Just as the Lord credited righteousness to Abraham on the basis of his faith, so righteousness will be given to sinners (you and me and whomever we speak to) today through their individual faith (Romans. 4:23-24). Through faith, not by virtue of works; therefore, we are dependent on Jesus Christ for salvation, not on our actions. God makes it clear in Scripture that He, through Christ, has made provision so we may be saved:

"For it is by grace you have been saved, through faith—and this not from yourselves, it is the gift of God—not by works, so that no one can boast"(Ephesians 2:8-9).

Again in Romans 11:6:

> *"And if by grace, then it is no longer by works; if it were, grace would no longer be grace."*

And again in Titus 3:4-7:

> *"But when the kindness and love of God our Savior appeared, he saved us, not because of righteous things we had done, but because of his mercy. He saved us through the washing of rebirth and renewal by the Holy Spirit, whom he poured out on us generously through Jesus Christ our Savior, so that, having been justified by his grace, we might become heirs having the hope of eternal life"*

And, still again in 1 John 5:10-13 Scripture declares:

> *"Anyone who believes in the Son of God has this testimony in his heart. Anyone who does not believe God has made him out to be a liar, because he has not believed the testimony God has given about his Son. And this is the testimony: God has given us eternal life, and this life is in his Son. He who has the Son has life; he who does not have the Son of God does not have life. I write these things to you who believe in the name of the Son of God so that you may know that you have eternal life."*

PEACE WITH GOD

When we realize that only the perfect Christ can save us and not our own good lives, then we will experience peace with God. Many Christians have no peace because they continue to trust in their own works, actions, and beliefs rather than accepting the sacrifice of Jesus. Isaiah says in 64:6:

> *"All of us have become like one who is unclean, and all our righteous acts are like filthy rags . . . "*

We will enjoy peace with our God to the degree we permit Christ to be our Savior (Romans 5:1). Read Romans 5:8-10 again and notice:

> *"Christ died for us . . . justified by his blood . . . saved from God's wrath through him . . . saved through his life!"*

We Christians must be fully convinced of and boldly claim the credited righteousness God gives us through his Son! When we look at our lives, our past sins, we may feel hopeless, just as Abraham did when God told him he would have a son. Nevertheless, he believed God and acted on his belief. Like Abraham, we must be strengthened in our faith, and give glory to God! We need to regularly ask ourselves, "Is anything too hard for the Lord?!" When we understand this good news, we then have something to share! It is like a homeless, starving person finding a source of food and shelter that can never be depleted. We must pass it on.

Questions:

1. Why was Abraham referred to as a "friend of God?"

2. What do I need to do to be a friend of God?

3. What must I possess to be at peace with God and myself?

4. Describe what God has provided for us to be saved.

CHAPTER 12

And this is the testimony: God has given us eternal life, and this life is in his Son. He who has the Son has life; he who does not have the Son of God does not have life. I write these things to you who believe in the name of the Son of God so that you may know that you have eternal life. (1 John 5:11-13)

DO YOU KNOW YOU ARE SAVED?

Do you suppose that one who believes the promises of God, who is strong in faith, fully persuaded God has power to do what he has promised, and has accepted the gift of salvation, will express doubt about whether he or she is saved? Will such a one ever say, "I don't know for sure I'm saved, but I hope I am"? The Word declares, *"There is now no condemnation for those who are in Christ Jesus . . . " (Romans 8:1).* Can I deny that promise if I am in Christ, having the faith of Abraham as I walk according to the Spirit?

The answer to the question of whether one is saved should be an emphatic *"Yes!"* by those that are *in Christ.* To answer this way is not to boast that I am righteous in and of myself, but to simply affirm I have accepted the free gift of God—salvation through Jesus Christ. His righteousness is my righteousness! I am *saved by his life,* not by my own.

To express doubt about my salvation reveals that I believe the life and sacrifice of Jesus to be insufficient or it could be that I am not living before God with wholehearted obedience. God's word tells us definitely *when* we transitioned from darkness into light: it occurred *when* we *"wholeheartedly obeyed the form of teaching,"* we were then *"set free from sin"* by acceptance of the death, burial, and resurrection of Jesus for my sins (1 Corinthians 15:1-4).

I initially demonstrated my belief in Jesus the Son of God by my death to sin (repentance), then by burying that dead man in water (baptism) to be raised to new life. I was put into Christ by obeying Scripture, and as long as I continue to *yield* to the Spirit, I can claim the promise of *"no condemnation."*

We must understand that baptism is not a work of merit. Scriptural baptism is not what some call "baptismal regeneration." We are not immersed to *earn* salvation, but to *accept* salvation. It is like the trillion dollar check that you had to fill out and deposit to make it yours. You didn't earn it, you simply accepted it. We wouldn't earn redemption even if we worked for a trillion years. Salvation cannot be bought by our works (2 Timothy. 1:9; Titus 3:5), but is freely given by God's grace and mercy (Ephesians 2:8-9).

Paul affirms in Galatians 5:6:

> *"For in Christ Jesus neither circumcision nor uncircumcision has any value. The only thing that counts is faith expressing itself through love."*

Although we're not saved by our deeds, a person cannot be saved and *refuse* to work (Ephesians. 2:10; Philippians 2:12-13). As Paul mentioned in Galatians 5:6, faith does *express itself!*

STRATEGIES FOR OVERCOMING OBJECTIONS

- You may ask: "God has offered the gift of salvation in his Son. You can't earn it, but if you fully believe, he will give you this gift through Christ. Will you accept his gift and be saved?"

Possible answer: "I want to, but I just don't believe I can live the Christian life." Note: This response indicates that person is still looking to self instead of to Christ.

Your response: "If it were up to us, to depend upon our own power, I'm sure we could not live a godly life. But God promises his Spirit will enable us." (c.f. Romans 8:13, 16, 26; John. 8:31-32, 36. Note also Acts 2:38; 5:32; Galatians 4:6)

****

- You may ask: "Are you *in* Christ?'

Possible answer: "Yes, I was baptized as a baby."

Your response: "Have you been buried in baptism with Christ to express faith in his death, burial and resurrection for your sins?" Note: Something is always required prior to baptism. (c.f. Matthew 28:19-20; Mark 16:16; Acts 2:38; 8:35-39) A baby cannot meet the prerequisites of baptism.

****

■ You may ask: "Are you in Christ?"

Possible answer: "Yes, I was baptized by the Holy Spirit into Christ."

Your response: Point out that Ephesians 4:5 teaches there is ONE baptism.

What is the ONE baptism?

Matthew 28:19-20

1. This baptism was to be *administered by men* on the authority of the Father, the Son and the Holy Spirit. Only God can baptize with the Holy Spirit.

2. It will last until the end of the age.

3. This baptism is to be in water.

****

- You are asked: "Why doesn't Romans 10:9-10 say anything about baptism? Those verses say if we believe with our heart and confess with our mouth we will be saved."

> *That if you confess with your mouth, "Jesus is Lord," and believe in your heart that God raised him from the dead, you will be saved. For it is with your heart that you believe and are justified, and it is with your mouth that you confess and are saved.*

Your response: What will a person do who believes "with all his heart" that Jesus is Lord? He will obey him and openly confess him. The people of Acts 2 did not question Peter when he told them what they needed to do.

Questions:

1. Can I know that I am in a right relationship with God (saved)? If so, how?

2. What does it mean to be "in Christ?"

3. The gospel is the best news that has ever been announced, so what keeps us from sharing it with others?

4. What are some reasons you have or that you have heard from others, for not sharing the gospel?

5. Discuss Galatians 5:6: *"For in Christ Jesus neither circumcision nor uncircumcision has any value. The only thing that counts is faith expressing itself through love."*

CHAPTER 13

Although he was a son, he learned obedience from what he suffered and, once made perfect, he became the source of eternal salvation for all who obey him. (Hebrews 5:8-9)

TEACHING THEM
TO OBSERVE EVERYTHING

Realize that God is not finished with someone when we baptize him. That person is now a newborn baby in the family of God (1 Peter 2:2). We don't expect a baby to walk or talk in the delivery room; neither can we expect it of one newly born into God's family. Just as the physical baby will die without adequate care, so the spiritual baby will not thrive unless we nurture him. Our God commands that we not only teach and baptize, but also teach anyone baptized to *"obey everything I have commanded you"* (Matthew 28:20). He or she must be lovingly brought to maturity!

CARING FOR NEW CHRISTIANS

Association is so important to the new convert. Involvement with other Christians is vital! As someone has pointed out, the banana that leaves the bunch is the one that gets peeled! New Christians need a fellowship group. A home study group is a great way to facilitate growth, and integrate newborn believers into the lives of brothers and sisters in the body. If you don't feel you can lead such a group, seek out someone who can.

- Stay in touch with the new Christian. Invite him into your home, and to activities you normally engage in with the church you attend.

- Ask other couples in the church family to give special attention to the new Christian.

- Seek out someone to be a big "brother" or "sister" to the new Christian; someone who loves the Lord and is dependable and trustworthy.

- Arrange a time when you can study further with him. He may also be interested in Bible correspondence courses.

- Provide transportation if you must, to be sure he attends church worship services.

- Involvement is a key to his growth. Work with him over time to help him discover and use his talents for the Lord. Acquaint him with the congregation's classes, ministries, events, etc. Christians were busy serving God in the early church!

Don't Forget to Just Ask!

Sometimes we miss opportunities to share Christ because we make it too complicated. Cindy, a Christian and a teacher, had been taking one of her former high school students with her to church services for several months. She had put in a word for Jesus from time to time and even shown him the baptistery in the church building. Cindy's efforts to reach her student were good, but, he had yet to surrender his life to Christ.

When a new evangelist moved in, Cindy mentioned her student to him one Wednesday night at Bible class, pointing Josh out in the crowd. Anthony promptly engaged him in conversation, had a Bible study involving the Roman's approach, and within a short time, Josh was in the baptistery, ready to be immersed.

Cindy, though very happy with Josh's decision, was puzzled. "I've been bringing Josh to church with me for months now, and I've talked to him many times about Jesus and how his life would be as a Christian. I don't understand, how did this happen?" she asked Anthony after Josh's baptism.

He smiled, "I just asked . . . "

Cindy walked away scratching her head. Later she told Anthony, "You know, out of all the times I talked with this young man, I never *just asked*!"

Just ask.

LOOKING BACK . . .

The year was 1975. The leadership at the Central Church of Christ took seriously Jesus' command to *"preach the gospel to every creature" (Mark 16:15)*. We decided to begin obeying the Lord in our city of 110,000 residents, knocking on over 10,000 doors with the help of college campaign workers and other friends. A tent meeting concluded the campaign—I met Gary for the first time one night underneath this tent.

At the conclusion of one nightly service, Cory, a campaign worker, and I were gathering up song books when I noticed a guy still seated in the empty tent. I walked over, and after introductions he asked, "Did I understand from your sermon that a person is to be baptized after he believes?" I assumed he was referring to Mark 16:16, in which Jesus said: *"Whoever believes and is baptized will be saved, but whoever does not believe will be condemned."*

I assured him he was exactly right, to which he responded, "Then that's what I want to do!" Cory, Gary and I drove immediately to the Central Church building and Gary was immersed.

Coming up out of the baptistery, our new brother dried his face and commented, "Now I have a problem!"

"How can you have a problem?" I asked, puzzled. "You've just been united with Christ, your sins are forgiven, you're on your way to heaven—and you have a problem?" He explained, "Yes. You see, my wife has this thing about religion. This might just wreck our marriage!"

Cory and I suggested at the same time, "Let's pray." We joined hands, praying fervently for God to protect Gary's marriage, and open his wife's heart.

The following night Gary was back, this time with his wife, Zoe, and their dear friends, Larry and Deidra. Imagine my surprise when Zoe came forward at the invitation, requesting to also be baptized! Gary later enlightened us about the events of the prior evening.

Arriving home, he opened the front door to find his wife sitting on the couch, tearfully waiting up for him. They looked directly at one another. The first words that tumbled from her mouth were, "Gary, why don't you talk to me about the Bible anymore?" Recovering his composure, he excitedly shared with her his surrender to Jesus Christ.

Eventually Gary and Zoe relocated; Gary earned a degree in Bible, after which they began full time ministry. After working for many years in the Midwest with several different churches, they moved to Tampa, Florida, where they've served the Bay Area Church of Christ for over 15 years. Many, many people are heaven-bound as a result of Gary and Zoe's zeal for the Lord. Three grown children—Jami, Josh and Zach, and their spouses (all of whom are Christians) complete their family.

A Surprise and a Delight

Sitting in the living room of our home one evening, my wife handed me a storage box and said, "If you want to experience some nostalgia look through this." Out of curiosity I began to search through the items in the box and found Father's Day cards from my children, notes from my wife and various other things dating back over 30 years. I also found a small envelope with a 37 cent stamp post marked in 2002. The return address showed Hallsville, TX 75650. I removed a letter and it read as follows:

> *Dear Jim,*
>
> *I take great pleasure in writing to tell you of the success my wife & I have had reaching the lost using the Romans Approach to salvation.*
>
> *A friend gave me a R.A. Tape in 1982. Since then the Lord, my wife & I have converted more than 50 souls using it.*
>
> *I am so thankful for the tape you recently gave me. I promise it will be used. I'm so grateful for brothers like you who have the knowledge of God's salvation plan & the ability to organize it in a way that faith, the love of God, the origin of sin, God's grace, His salvation plan & Church membership can all be taught by nearly anyone.*

My prayer is, may God bless & keep you in all that you do.
In Brotherly love,
Gene Tolar

I have shared the letter just as it was written. You can listen to the tape that Gene is referring to here: http://campusministryunited.com/Audio/RomansApproachLive.mp3 I am delighted that God has used this study to bring hundreds to Christ. The gospel is the power of God for salvation. The study from Romans presents the truth in such a way that people who are far away from God can understand it. God describes our part in sharing the gospel message in this way:

> *"We have this treasure in jars of clay to show that this all-surpassing power is from God and not from us"*
> *(2 Corinthians 4:7).*

I pray that God will bless you richly as you explore this study!

FOCUSING ON JESUS

When I witnessed the power of just presenting Jesus as my brother John had done with Gerry, I was so excited I just had to try this approach with someone! I made a list of those who had never accepted the Lord, but who came with their Christian spouses to our congregation. After making appointments with them, I went to their homes, engaged in a little polite conversation, and then got down to why I was there.

I said, "I know you've been attending services with your family for some time. You've heard me preach many sermons; you know that the invitation to accept Christ as Lord has been extended after each lesson."

Then I would pose the same question my brother asked of our brother-in-law, Gerry: "Do you believe Jesus Christ is the Son of God?" The answer was, in almost every case, "Yes." My next question would be, "Would you like to receive Christ as your Lord and Savior today?" Over a six-week period 16 individuals accepted Christ as their Lord and Savior by being baptized.

We moved to Davenport, Iowa, in 1973 to work with the Central Church of Christ. During the next two and one-half years, over 200 put on the Lord in baptism, through simply focusing on Jesus Christ.

CHRISTIANS SOW THE SEED, GOD GIVES THE INCREASE

Jesus said, "This is what the kingdom of God is like. A man scatters seed on the ground. Night and day, whether he sleeps or gets up, the seed sprouts and grows, though he does not know how. All by itself the soil produces grain—first the stalk, then the head, then the full kernel in the head. As soon as the grain is ripe, he puts the sickle to it, because the harvest has come" (Mark 4:26-29).

Paul said, "I planted the seed, Apollos watered it, but God made it grow." (1 Corinthians 3:6)

Questions:

1. Do you pray for people who do not have a relationship with Christ?

2. What do you see as important steps to keep a new Christian in fellowship with Christ?

3. Take a few minutes to tell your story.

4. Can you name one or more individuals who are unsaved that you could "just ask" about their relationship with Christ?

5. Do you have a message to share when the opportunity to present the gospel comes up?

6. Would you prefer to have a GPS or a personal guide? Which of these metaphors does Christ best represent?

Notes

SOME CLOSING THOUGHTS

As the words of a popular hymn express it: "Tis done, the great transactions done; I am my Lord's, and he is mine!"

Having been drawn by the Father, you have given your life to Jesus Christ (John. 6:44-45). You are no longer your own, you have been bought with the precious blood of the Lamb (1 Corinthians 6:19-20; 1 Peter 1:18-23). Now you are "in Christ" (Romans 8:1; Galatians 3:27) and Jesus is in you. You have been rescued *"from the dominion of darkness and brought into the kingdom of the Son he loves" (Colossians 1:13)*. What a fellowship! What a joy divine!

Surely you know others who need the gospel of Jesus; perhaps a brother, sister, mother, dad or friend who has never accepted Jesus as Lord. You may be the only one willing to contact these dear ones. If you do not share the gospel, they may never hear.

The Bible is clear: those who die outside of Christ are lost. People who are lost will go to hell, a place prepared especially for the "devil and his angels" (Matthew 25:41)

There is no salvation apart from Christ:

> *Acts 4:12 "Salvation is found in no one else, for there is no other name under heaven given to men by which we must be saved."*

Hell is an awful place. It is described as a place of fire and torment (Matthew 25:41, 46), and as a place where there will be "wailing and gnashing of teeth" (Matthew 13:41, 42, 49, 50). Jesus said it is better to go through life with a crippled body than to go to hell (Matthew 5:29-30; 18:8). A very compelling motive we have for sharing the gospel of Christ is to keep people out of hell fire!

Consider the words of Paul in 2 Thessalonians 1:7-9:

> *This will happen when the Lord Jesus is revealed from heaven in blazing fire with his powerful angels. He will punish those who do not know God and do not obey the gospel of our Lord Jesus. They will be punished with everlasting destruction and shut out from the presence of the Lord and from the majesty of his power.*

This is a life or death issue. Scripture is clear. Those who do not obey the gospel will be lost from God forever. The gospel of

Jesus has the power to rescue people from the grip of sin and destruction, but God is depending on us to share that message.

This study, and the personal experiences that are shared, are designed to motivate and enable you to reach the lost! Using your Bible, take time to immerse yourself in this timeless message from the book of Romans, putting it into your own heart first. Underline the passages in your Bible used in the study. There is an outline of the Roman's study at the end of this book. At the same time pray for an open door to speak the mystery of Christ, asking God to give you wisdom to *"proclaim it clearly" (Colossians 4:4)*. When the door of someone's heart opens, present the gospel.

Notes

ADDENDUM

THE ROMANS APPROACH TO WINNING THE LOST

Intro: Have you reached the point in your spiritual life where you can say with confidence, "I know if I died right now I would go to heaven?" YOU CAN HAVE THAT CONFIDENCE!

A.   **In this study of Romans we are taking the heart of the message out of the book.**

I.   **Romans 4**

    A.   **Romans 4:4-5**
        1.   **Illustration: trillion Dollars. YOU CANNOT EARN WHAT YOU CANNOT EARN.**

    B.   **Romans 4:20-21**
        1.   **Abraham an example Genesis 12:1-4**

    C.   **Romans 4:22-25**
        1.   **"Imputed" righteousness.**

2. Matthew 22:11-14

3. Illustration: Shepherd and sheep.

D. Romans 4:25
   1. Historical Fact!! Cannot be changed. Can only be accepted or rejected.

II. Romans 5

A. Romans 5:1

B. Romans 5:6, 8-10 In these verses is God's focus on the sinner and sinner's obligation to Him, or is His focus on Christ and the provision of salvation He has provided to us in his son??

Where is God's focus? Obviously, it is on what God has done for us through Christ. Your salvation was paid for by Jesus "at just the right time" while you were "powerless" and "ungodly" (vs. 6), and a "sinner" (vs. 8) "under God's wrath" (vs. 9), an enemy of God (vs. 10). We are not saved by our life (deeds we have done or will do), but BY HIS LIFE (vs. 10b)!)

C. Romans 5:12 Who was the one man that brought sin into the world?

ADAM

↓

SINNED

↓

DEATH

Death was a consequence of Adam's sin and death was passed on to all of Adam's descendents. You and I will die because of Adam's sin. Adam was "a pattern of the one who was to come." 5:14b)

D. **Romans 5:15-17 How many times is the word "gift" used in these 4 verses? Define a gift? Can you earn a gift? Can you pay for a gift?**

Compare what these verses teach to Romans 5:12:

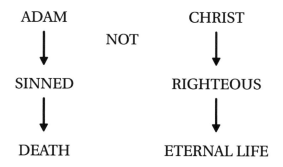

ADAM		CHRIST
↓	NOT	↓
SINNED		RIGHTEOUS
↓		↓
DEATH		ETERNAL LIFE

E. Romans 5:18

   1. What was the "one trespass" that brought condemnation?

   2. What was the "one act of righteousness" that brings life?

F. Romans 5:19

   1. Whose disobedience made many sinners?

   2. Whose obedience will make many righteous?

G. Romans 5:20

   1. Can sin overpower God's grace?

Do you agree with this summary?

1. We cannot earn our salvation?

2. If we are made righteous, it will be Christ's righteousness that makes us righteous?

3. Salvation is a "gift" from God?

4. Where there is sin, God's grace is sufficient to cover it? Sin cannot overpower God's grace!

Someone says, "I know what I will do! I will accept the gift of salvation and live like I want to, because sin cannot overpower the grace of God. I will just sin and let grace cover me."

III. **ROMANS 6 (Throughout this chapter Paul is answering the argument of, "I'll sin and let grace cover me." IT WON'T WORK!)**

    A. **Romans 6:1-2**
        1. **What do you do with someone who has died?**

    B. **Romans 6:3-4**
        People are buried because they have died to sin.

    C. **Romans 6:12-13**
        1. **Key word is "yield" or "offer." Means to completely surrender, without struggle.**

    D. **Romans 6:14 (Romans 5:20 does apply to those who are striving to live for God, even though they fail at times.)**

    E. **Romans 6:15**
        1. **If a person says, "I have accepted Christ, but I'm going to live like I want to," what is that person yielding to?**

    F. **Romans 6:17-18 (What can wash away my sin? When are my sins forgiven?)**
        1. **With the whole heart.**

        2. **Obeyed.**

        3. **"the form of teaching."**

    4.   KJV "being THEN set free from sin."

G.   Romans 6:23

    1.   What are the wages of sin?

    2.   What is the "free gift" of God?

    (Can you pay your own sin-debt?)

IV. ROMANS 7

A.   Romans 7:14-20 (The problem is not with the perfect law of God, it is with US.)

B.   Romans 7:21-23

C.   Romans 7:24-25 (Who will deliver us from this "body of death?" NOT what!)

V. ROMANS 8

A.   Romans 8:1

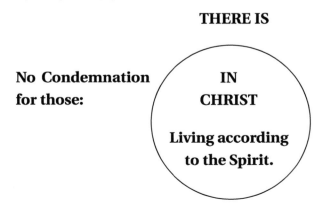

THERE IS

No Condemnation for those:

IN
CHRIST

Living according to the Spirit.

B. HOW DOES A PERSON GET INTO CHRIST? Read:
Romans 6:3-4; Galatians 3:26-28

VI. FROM ACTS.

A. Acts 2

1. Acts 2:22-24
   What was the message that Peter preached?
   Where was his focus?

2. Acts 32, 36

3. Acts 2:37 What was the hearer's response?
   Why?

4. Acts 2:38-39 What did Peter instruct the people
   to do? Why? What do you do with someone who
   has died?

5. Acts 2:41-42 What did the hearers who accepted
   the word do?

6. Acts 2:47 What did God do in the way of blessing
   them?

B. Acts 8

1. Acts 8:26-39

What did Philip preach to the Ethiopian? (vs. 35)

Why did the Ethiopian want to be baptized? (vs. 36)

Why did both Philip and the Ethiopian go down into the water? (vs. 38)

NOTE: Those who have accepted Christ will do what he says! 1 John 2:3-6; Luke 6:46; John 14:15, 23.

Illustrations/Helps used during the study:

Trillion Dollars. How much is a trillion dollars? If you made $10 per hour and worked a 40 hour week ($400 per week) do you know how long it would take you to earn a trillion dollars? Over 100,000 years! Do you think you could ever earn a trillion dollars? You cannot earn what you cannot earn. But somebody offers you a trillion dollars. All you have to do is sign your name where it says, "Pay to the order of _____, and it yours. You sign your name and deposit it into your account, so now it is yours, but did you earn it?? Obviously, all you did was accept it.

Shepherd and Sheep. A shepherd discovers an orphaned lamb and he wants it to live. He tries everything at his disposal to get it to eat. Nothing works. He takes the lamb to a mother sheep to see if she will adopt it, but she will have nothing to do with it. In desperation he takes the mother sheep's own offspring, her own little lamb, and slaughters it. He skins it out, taking its hide and draping it over the orphaned lamb. He then brings the orphaned lamb to the mother sheep, which had previously rejected it. Smelling the scent of her own offspring, she adopts the orphaned lamb. This is exactly what God has done for us with Christ. (Isaiah 53:4-7).

Romans 5:12. If I choose to gamble, bet my house, car and next years salary and loose, I am the one who sins, but my whole family will suffer as a consequence. Adam sinned, but the entire human family suffers as a consequence. Death is a consequence.

Yield or offer. The Greeks used this word to describe what happened in a wrestling match when one opponent, after throwing the other opponent to the mat, had him to "give up" without further resistance. When resistance ceased the wrestler "yielded" or "offered" himself to his opponent. As long as we resist sin and offer ourselves to God sin cannot dominate us, "because we are not under law, but under grace."

In Christ. The promise of "no condemnation" is for those who are "in Christ living according to the Spirit." To live according to the Spirit is to "yield" to God; follow the Word of God.

If you were informed that terrorist were about to attack your city, but you can escape destruction by getting into a SECURE SHELTER. Likely you would ask directions to the shelter and ask, "How do I get into it?" There is no destruction "in Christ." The question is, "How do I get into Christ?" That question is answered in Romans 6:3-4. It is also addressed in Galatians 3:26-28.

Acts references. The examples of conversion in Acts 2 and 8 are used to corroborate the teachings of Paul in Romans. You have three different NT preachers (Paul, Peter, and Philip) who preach on three different occasions, in varied circumstances to diverse audiences, but they all preach the same message (Jesus Christ, His death for our sins, His burial in the grave, and His resurrection).

Let those that you study with answer the questions relating to these conversion accounts so they will see the application from what they have learned in Romans, and also make application to their own lives.

Notes

Notes

Notes

Notes